COOL SCIENCE

SPORTS SCIENCE

John Perritano

mc Marshall Cavendish
Benchmark
New York

This edition first published in 2011
by Marshall Cavendish Benchmark.

Marshall Cavendish Benchmark
99 White Plains Road
Tarrytown, NY 10591
www.marshallcavendish.us

Published by Marshall Cavendish Benchmark
An imprint of Marshall Cavendish Corporation

Other Marshall Cavendish Offices:
Marshall Cavendish International (Asia) Private Limited, 1 New Industrial Road, Singapore 536196
• Marshall Cavendish International (Thailand) Co Ltd. 253 Asoke, 12th Flr, Sukhumvit 21 Road,
Klongtoey Nua, Wattana, Bangkok 10110, Thailand • Marshall Cavendish (Malaysia) Sdn Bhd,
Times Subang, Lot 46, Subang Hi-Tech Industrial Park, Batu Tiga, 40000 Shah Alam,
Selangor Darul Ehsan, Malaysia

Marshall Cavendish is a trademark of Times Publishing Limited

Library of Congress Cataloging-in-Publication Data
Perritano, John.
Sports science / John Perritano.
p. cm. — (Cool science)
Includes index.
ISBN 978-1-60870-081-3
1. Sports sciences—Juvenile literature. I. Title.
GV558.P38 2011
613.7'1—dc22
2009053777

Created by Q2AMedia
Series Editor: Bonnie Dobkin
Art Director: Harleen Mehta
Client Service Manager: Santosh Vasudevan
Project Manager: Kumar Kunal
Line Artists: Narender Kasana, Vinay Kumar
Coloring Artists: Danish Zaidi, Nazia Zaidi, Madhavi Poddar, Rohit Sharma
Photo research: Debabrata Sen, Nivisha Sinha
Designers: Cheena Yadav, Neha Kaul

The photographs in this book are used by permission and through the courtesy of:

Cover: Wayne Geisler/Shutterstock; Istockphoto; Istockphoto
Half title: Eric Limón/Istockphoto

4: Shaun Best/Reuters; 5: Hkratky/Dreamstime; 6: Duncan Walker/Istockphoto; 7t: Florida Stock/Shutterstock;
7c: Arthur Kwiatkowski/Istockphoto; 7b: Haessly Photography/Shutterstock; 8: James Steidl/Shutterstock; 9: Sven Hoppe/
Shutterstock; 10: Jonathan Hayward/The Canadian Press/AP Photo; 11: Dominic Ebenbichler/Reuters; 12l: Richard Paul
Kane/Shutterstock; 12r: Stephen Mcsweeny/Shutterstock; 14: Mark Lennihan/AP Photo; 16: Martti Kainulainen/
Rex Features; 17t: Arenacreative/Shutterstock; 17b: American Honda Motor Co., Inc.; 18l: Eugene Buchko/Shutterstock;
18r: Wayne Geisler/Shutterstock; 19l: R. Gino Santa Maria/Shutterstock; 19r: AP Photo; 20: Darren Staples/Reuters;
21: Todd Korol/Reuters; 22: Douglas C. Pizac/AP Photo; 24: Olivier Maire/AP Photo; 25: Dani Vincek/Shutterstock;
26: Marc Duncan/AP Photo; 27: Richard Paul Kane/Shutterstock; 28: Konstantin Komarov/Shutterstock; 29: Jonathan
Larsen/Shutterstock; 30: David J Phillip/AP Photo; 31: Jacqueline Abromeit/Shutterstock; 32: David J Phillip/AP Photo;
33: Richardpross/Big Stock Photo; 34: Richard Paul Kane/Shutterstock; 35: Bob Jordan/AP Photo; 36: Kashif Masood/
AP Photo; 38: Jonathan Larsen/Shutterstock; 39t: Chad McDermott/Shutterstock; 39b: Rob Byron/Shutterstock;
40: Wolfgang Rattay/Reuters; 41: Dmitry Yashkin/Shutterstock; 42: Jiang Dao Hua/Shutterstock; 43t: Photogolfer/
Shutterstock; 43b: Mike Liu/Shutterstock, 44: Orange Line Media/Shutterstock; 45: Philip Morton/Sports Interactive Media

Q2AMedia Art Bank: 11, 13, 15, 20, 23, 25, 36, 37

Printed in Malaysia (T)

135642
9012

CONTENTS

Sports Meets Science

The bases are loaded. Albert Pujols digs into the batter's box. The St. Louis Cardinals slugger gives Mets pitcher Sean Green a "give me your best pitch" look.

Green goes into his windup and lets the ball fly. Pujols swings a mighty swing. The bat connects with the ball, which soars to the deepest part of left-centerfield. The announcer cries: "It's well hit! It's gone! Grannnnnnnd slammmmmmmmmm for Albert Pujols, his second home run today!"

With that swing, the Cardinals' slugger ties the National League single-season grand slam record. Even more amazing, he's the only player in baseball history to have managed at least a .300 batting average, thirty home runs, one hundred RBIs and ninety-nine runs scored in each of his first eight big-league seasons.

While most people would consider Pujols an amazing athlete, he's much more. He's also an amazing specimen of science.

Albert Pujols is considered one of the best all-around players in the game today.

If you're a fan of baseball, soccer, football, or any other sport, you're also a fan of science. Behind every pitch, every kick, and every forward pass are such scientific concepts as **gravity**, **biomechanics**, motion, and kinetic energy.

Understanding certain scientific concepts can make an athlete stronger, faster, and more agile. Other laws of science can improve a player's skills and technique. Science can make a coach more effective, help a manager choose the right equipment, and even fool the opposing team. As for spectators, knowing the science that's at work makes an athlete's accomplishments even more amazing!

Everything from this player's kick to the movement of the football depends on a combination of scientific principles.

NEWTON'S NOTIONS OF MOTION

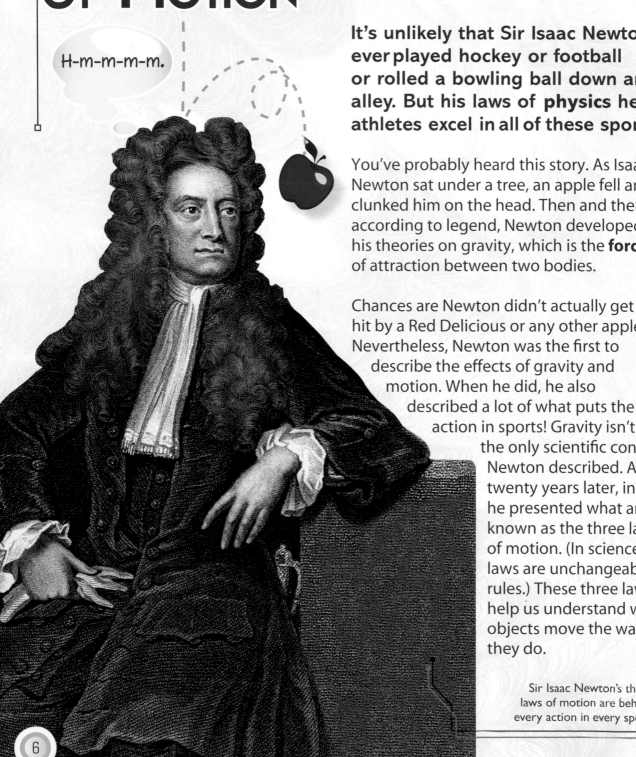

H-m-m-m-m.

It's unlikely that Sir Isaac Newton ever played hockey or football or rolled a bowling ball down an alley. But his laws of physics help athletes excel in all of these sports.

You've probably heard this story. As Isaac Newton sat under a tree, an apple fell and clunked him on the head. Then and there, according to legend, Newton developed his theories on gravity, which is the **force** of attraction between two bodies.

Chances are Newton didn't actually get hit by a Red Delicious or any other apple. Nevertheless, Newton was the first to describe the effects of gravity and motion. When he did, he also described a lot of what puts the action in sports! Gravity isn't the only scientific concept Newton described. About twenty years later, in 1686, he presented what are known as the three laws of motion. (In science, laws are unchangeable rules.) These three laws help us understand why objects move the way they do.

Sir Isaac Newton's three laws of motion are behind every action in every sport.

Newton's Three Laws of Motion

NEWTON'S FIRST LAW

An object in motion will remain in motion unless acted upon by an outside force. An object at rest will remain at rest. In other words, a moving object keeps moving. An object that's sitting still, stays still.

NEWTON'S SECOND LAW

This law is a bit more complicated. It describes the relationship between force, **mass**, and acceleration. The mathematical formula is written as **F=ma**. What does this mean? Simply put, it means that the heavier an object is, the more force and speed are needed to move it. Think about it. Have you ever taken a running start at something in order to move or break through it? If so, you've used Newton's second law.

NEWTON'S THIRD LAW

According to this law, for every action, there is an equal and opposite reaction. For example, what would happen if two balls rolled into each other? When they hit, each would bounce backward again. A similar reaction causes a baseball to pop off a bat when the two connect.

Bowling
Rolling Down the Lane

If you have ever gone bowling, you know the drill: roll the ball down the lane and knock over as many pins as possible. As you do, you'll be following Newton's three laws of motion!

First, throw the bowling ball. The heavier the ball and the harder you throw it, the faster it rolls and the more force it will have. That's Newton's second law: **F=ma**. Next, the ball rolls down the alley. It continues to travel at the same speed until some other force—the **friction** from the floor, the ten pins, and the wall behind the pins—slows it down or stops it. That's Newton's first law. And then what happens? With skill and luck, you knock down some pins! Following Newton's third law, they fly away with a force equal and opposite to the force of the ball as it hits them.

THE SCIENCE ADVANTAGE

When bowlers throw a "hook," they try to make the ball curve down the alley to strike between the head pin and one of the pins closest to it. This angle helps distribute the force of the ball evenly among the ten pins.

A good "hook" takes a lot of science! After the backswing, gravity pulls the ball down. The bowler then adds his or her energy to push the ball forward and give it a slight spin. The ball is released on the side of the lane, where there is less oil and more friction. As the spinning ball grips the boards, it begins to curve. If all conditions are right . . . STRIKE!

Ice Hockey
Blades vs. Ice

NHL players can reach speeds of more than 20 miles (32 kilometers) per hour on the ice. Gravity and friction are two reasons they can move so fast.

A spray of ice shows the force with which these skaters dig their blades into the surface.

When a player wants to increase speed, he digs the blade of one of his skates into the ice, leans forward, and pushes. By leaning, the player allows gravity to begin pulling the upper body forward. Friction between the gripping blade and the slippery ice creates resistance. That resistance allows a player to push against the ice and adds to the forces moving him forward.

Similarly, friction helps players stop their forward movement. By pushing against the ice, skaters create resistance that slows them down or allows them to change direction.

THE SCIENCE ADVANTAGE

Wayne Gretzky is considered the greatest hockey player in history. But it wasn't speed, or Newton's laws, that made him so successful. Instead, he studied the angles a hockey puck takes during the game. By picturing exactly how the puck would bounce off the hockey stick, Gretzky could be in the right place at the right time to capture the puck and score, or to shovel a pass to a teammate.

Rowing

Three Laws in a Boat

When the eight-man Canadian rowing team won the gold medal at the 2008 Olympics in Beijing, China, Newton's laws were behind their victory.

The role of the first law is easy to see. The boat isn't going anywhere unless some force acts on it! To make this happen, the rowers dip the oars in the water and push the water backward. The speed of the boat depends on how much force the oars produce, and upon the mass of the boat and rowers. That's Newton's second law.

Newton also said that for every action there is an equal and opposite reaction. As the oars push against the water, they create a force that sends the boat in the opposite direction of the push. The oars push backward and the boat moves forward.

THE SCIENCE ADVANTAGE

Rowers used to prefer slimmer oars because those oars were easier to move through water. Slimmer oars, however, created less force to move the shell. Rowers then started using wider oars that require more strength to move. The wider oars, which are still in use today, create more force to move the shell. But instead of wood, rowers use oars made out of synthetic, or human-made, materials. They are lighter than wooden oars and easier to use.

Rowers coordinate the movement of their arms and legs, along with the position of their movable seats, to achieve the maximum amount of force between the oar blade and the water.

Shot Put
"Putting" It Out There

Newton's second law of motion (F=ma) was behind Tomasz Majewski's win in the 2008 Summer Olympics in Beijing, China. The Polish athlete threw a shot put 70.57 feet (21.51 meters), winning the gold for Poland.

Tomasz Majewski must know exactly when to release the shot put, and at what angle.

To get as much force behind a shot put toss as possible, a shot-putter needs both strength and technique. Strength is necessary to overcome the pull of gravity on the 16-pound (7.2-kilogram) steel ball. Technique involves finding just the right angle at which to release the shot put. The lower the angle, the less effort that is required for the athlete to move the shot put forward. But if the angle is too low, then gravity takes over again and the shot put drops to the ground too soon.

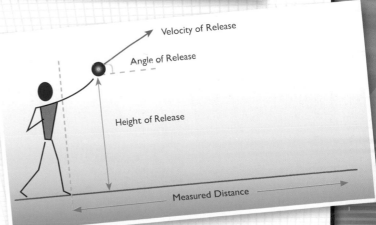

A successful shot put throw depends on the right combination of height, angle, and **velocity**.

Baseball

The Secret Behind the Swing

Hitting a baseball is one of the hardest things to do in sports. A professional batter has less than a quarter of a second to see the pitch and decide whether he wants to swing.

When the hitter decides to swing, he briefly moves backward and then "steps into the pitch." Stepping toward the pitch causes the batter's weight to shift from the back leg to the front leg.

As he steps into the pitch, the batter slightly turns his hips and shoulders and brings the bat forward. These movements provide the energy needed to drive the ball. At this point in the swing, the bat travels between 40 miles (64.4 km) to 80 miles (128.75 km) an hour.

TRAINER'S CORNER

Question: Is it important to follow through after hitting a pitch?

Answer: If you let go of the bat to run to first base the moment you hit the ball, the ball will travel just as far as if you followed through on the swing. Why is that? The bat-ball collision lasts only 1.5 milliseconds.

A pitcher's 90 mph (145 kph) fastball reaches home plate in 400 milliseconds.

The batter's swing takes 150 millseconds.

THE SCIENCE OF THE SWING

When a big-league pitcher throws a fastball, the batter has less than a quarter of a second to decide what to do.

Batter sees the ball and sends an image to the brain.

100 milliseconds

Brain processes the speed and location of the pitched ball.

75 milliseconds

Batter decides whether to swing, and then chooses a swing pattern.

50 milliseconds

Batter prepares to swing.

15 milliseconds

The batter swings. The bat must meet the ball within an inch of dead center, and at precisely the right moment.

150 milliseconds

The force with which a baseball connects with the bat depends on two things. The first is the speed of the pitch. The second is how fast a batter swings.

To hit a home run, the batter needs to hit the ball within an eighth of an inch of dead center. The ball and bat hit each other with exactly the same amount of force. Although these forces are equal and opposite, there is a net force on the ball that causes the ball to fly off the bat in the opposite direction from which it was pitched. It's Newton's third law in action.

THE BERNOULLI EFFECT

There are few shots in tennis like the devastating ace. No one knows this better than tennis stars like Andy Roddick and Serena Williams.

Known as the "Rocket Man," Andy Roddick holds the world record for the fastest serve in tennis. His serve travels at a blistering 155 miles (249.45 km) per hour. When a tennis ball is moving that fast, there is little time to react. Even the strongest opponents sometimes can't return the serve.

Serena Williams is another amazing athlete. Her fastest serve has been clocked at 127 miles, or 204.4 km, per hour. How do she, Roddick, and other players control their powerful hits? They hit the ball on a slant. This gives the ball topspin and causes it to curve downward more quickly than it normally would. When the ball hits the ground, it then pops back up faster than expected. The opponent swings and misses. Ace!

Serena Williams's average serve speed is 120 mph (193 kph).

The principle that causes a tennis ball to spin and move in a downward direction is the same one that allows an airplane to fly. That principle is known as the Bernoulli Effect, or the Bernoulli Principle. It was first described by Swiss physicist Daniel Bernoulli in the eighteenth century.

According to the Bernoulli Effect, air flows around an object at different speeds. The slower-moving air puts more pressure on the object than the faster-moving air. The object is then forced toward the faster-moving air.

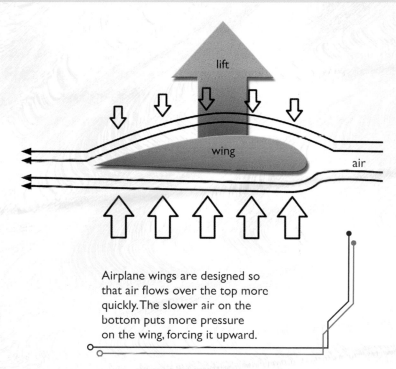

Airplane wings are designed so that air flows over the top more quickly. The slower air on the bottom puts more pressure on the wing, forcing it upward.

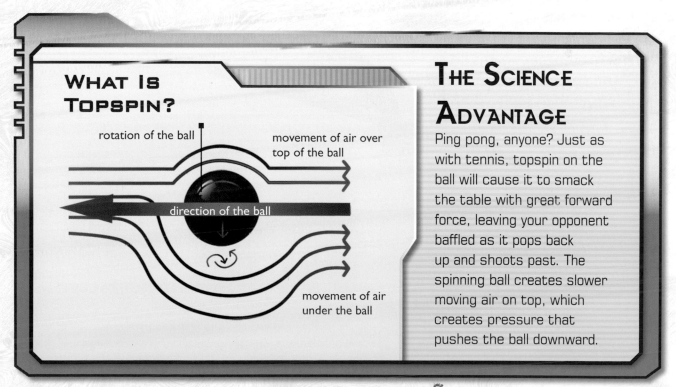

WHAT IS TOPSPIN?

rotation of the ball

movement of air over top of the ball

direction of the ball

movement of air under the ball

THE SCIENCE ADVANTAGE

Ping pong, anyone? Just as with tennis, topspin on the ball will cause it to smack the table with great forward force, leaving your opponent baffled as it pops back up and shoots past. The spinning ball creates slower moving air on top, which creates pressure that pushes the ball downward.

Ski Jump

Austria's Gregor Schlierenzauer, one of the top ski jumpers in the world, stands at the top of the snow-covered slide. He leaps forward and let's gravity start pulling him toward the bottom.

Then **air resistance** begins working against him. To overcome this, Schlierenzauer bends low at the knees and waist. He puts his arms behind him. Now there is less body surface for the air to push against. He may go faster than 60 miles per hour (97 kph)!

At the bottom of the slide, the World Cup champion jumps into the air, precisely angling his skis and body. The Bernoulli Effect takes over. Air rushes over the top of his body and skis to flow faster than the air below. Schlierenzauer gains lift and soars, staying in the air longer than seems possible!

With the right combination of factors, a skilled ski jumper can remain airborne for the length of a football field.

Car Racing

Bernoulli at the Wheel

There's one sport where athletes put the Bernoulli Effect in reverse—car racing. In this sport, athletes want to stay close to the ground, not fly off into the air!

In car racing, the faster a car travels, the greater the effect of lift. But when lift becomes too great, the car becomes hard to control. The key in countering lift is to create a downward force. To do that, engineers shape the bottom of the car like an upside down airplane wing. When air flows underneath a race car, the air is moving faster than the air above. This allows the car to grip the road a lot better.

Race cars are designed to slow the air traveling over the car, to keep downward force on the vehicle.

THE SCIENCE ADVANTAGE

Have you ever wondered why some race cars have crazy-looking "wings"? These wings are called spoilers. Engineers design these spoilers so air flows faster below the cars than above, which helps keep the tires on the road.

THE MAGNUS EFFECT

For years, scientists and baseball fans believed that the curveball was an optical illusion. After all, who could make a ball curve in midair?

Who threw the first curveball in baseball history? Some say it was Fred Goldsmith in the 1870s. Others say it was Candy Cummings in 1867. The truth is, no one knows for sure. What everyone does agree on, though, is that the pitch changed the history of the game. For years, scientists believed that a curveball wasn't real. Today, they know better.

Roy Halladay prepares to throw a curve ball by positioning his thumb and fingers as shown in the circle.

A curveball is a pitch that does not travel in a straight line. Instead, it curves to the right or left, and/or down. The Magnus Effect is the driving force behind the curveball.

Like the Bernoulli Effect, the Magnus Effect has to do with air pressure. Here's how it works on a thrown baseball. The pitcher first grips the ball with his middle and index fingers on or near the ball's stitching. He places his thumb underneath the ball.

As the pitcher begins his delivery, he twists the ball with his fingers and wrists as though he were turning a doorknob. This causes the ball to spin. As the spinning ball travels toward the batter, the stitching increases the amount of friction and creates higher air pressure on one side of the ball. The higher air pressure pushes the ball toward where the air pressure is the lowest, causing the ball to curve toward one side.

How a Curve Ball Curves

The stitching on a spinning baseball creates air pressure that forces the ball to one side.

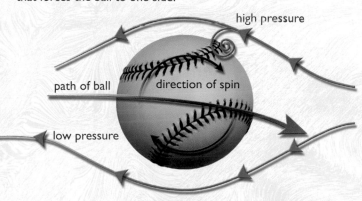

high pressure

path of ball   direction of spin

low pressure

direction of airflow across ball

Soccer

Bend It Like Beckham

It was October 6, 2001. England's David Beckham was given a free kick against Greece. The winner of the game would qualify for the World Cup.

Beckham placed the ball about 89 feet (27 meters) from the goal. He kicked the ball slightly off center, his left foot traveling at about 80 miles (129 km) per hour. The ball spun wildly. As it soared above the heads of the defensive line, it moved roughly 10 feet (3 m) to the left. The ball then slowed to 42 miles (68 km) per hour and dipped into the goal. The crowd went wild.

The Magnus Effect forced the spinning ball to curve. Gravity caused the ball to dip into the goal. And after that kick, thrilled fans turned "Bend it like Beckham" into a phrase known around the world.

This diagram shows the curve of Beckham's famous kick.

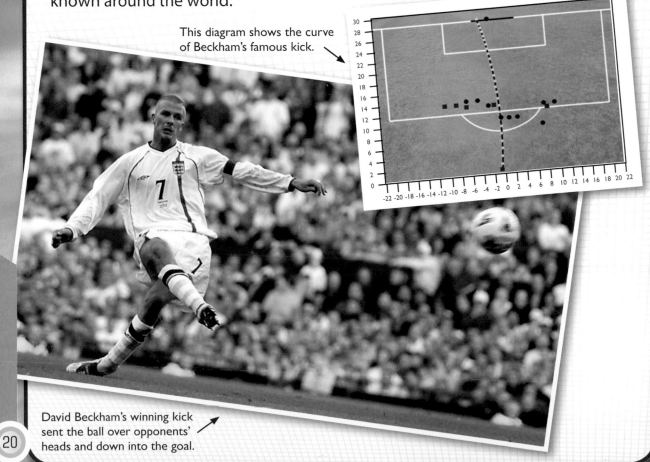

David Beckham's winning kick sent the ball over opponents' heads and down into the goal.

Golf
Slice It Up!

Golfers like Michelle Wie know how to use the Magnus Effect to its full advantage. When they're in a tough spot, like a hole with a curving fairway, they use a slice to make the ball go where they need it to.

Michelle Wie became a professional golfer when she was just fifteen years old.

In golf, a slice is when the ball curves in the shape of a banana. To hit a slice, a golfer like Wie visualizes where she wants the ball to go. She then faces the head of the club in the direction the ball needs to end up. Finally, she positions her body parallel to the line in which she wants the ball to begin traveling.

Whack! The club strikes the ball, causing it to spin sideways. The dimples on the ball create a high-pressure area. If the golfer is right-handed, the ball swerves from left to right. A good slice can win a match! An accidental one can lose it.

ENERGY: WHAT POTENTIAL!

It was the sixth game of the 1998 NBA Finals, and it was Michael Jordan's time to shine. The Chicago Bulls trailed the Utah Jazz 86-83. With 40 seconds left, Jordan scored a layup, cutting the Jazz's lead to one.

Jordan then did something many consider the greatest moment in NBA playoff history. He ran up the court against defender Byron Russell. With seconds left, Jordan made a desperate jump shot from inside the three-point line. He lifted the ball over his head, jumped slightly backward, and let the ball fly. The ball went through the hoop, and the Bulls beat the Jazz 87-86.

That amazing shot—one of many in Jordan's career—was made possible by the wonderful world of energy.

Michael Jordan makes the winning shot of the 1998 NBA finals.

COACH'S CORNER

Question: How important is backspin in making a jump shot?

Answer: When a ball with backspin hits the rim or backboard, the ball changes its **velocity** to go in the opposite direction of the spin. That change sends the ball back toward the net, making it likely that the ball will go into the basket.

What Is Energy?

Energy is the ability to do work or cause change. It is behind every sound, movement, and spark of light. When an object or organism exerts force on another object, some of its energy is transferred to that object.

Potential and kinetic energy make sports possible. Potential energy is energy that is stored until it needs to be used. Kinetic energy is the energy of motion. When Jordan made that jump shot against the Jazz, he created potential energy in the basketball by lifting it over his head. When he released the ball, the potential energy changed to kinetic energy and the ball sailed through the air and into the hoop. This kind of change also happens when a golfer takes a backswing, when a BMX biker begins to swoop down a ramp, and when a skier heads down a hill.

Potential energy changes to kinetic energy as this skier speeds down a slope.

PE: Potential Energy
KE: Kinetic Energy

Speed Skiing

Sanna Tidstrand of Sweden is one of the fastest women in the world. She's a speed skier who has raced down the hill at 150.74 miles (242.59 km) per hour.

Speed skiers like Tidstrand begin at the top of a hill that is 0.6 miles (1 kilometer) in length, and perfectly straight and smooth. As Tidstrand moves up that hill on a ski lift, she's gathering potential energy, moving against the pull of Earth's gravity. She positions herself at the start of the run and leaps forward.

Gravity then begins pulling her downhill, and the potential energy is converted into kinetic energy. As Tidstrand continues to rocket down the slope, the height of the slope and potential energy transform into kinetic energy and speed. Once Tidstrand reaches the bottom of the hill, her speed and kinetic energy have reached their maximum levels.

Sanna Tidstrand bends her body to reduce air resistance and allow gravity to pull her to the base of the hill as quickly as possible.

Fly Fishing
Energy on the Fly

When most people think of fishing, they think of sitting by a lake, lazily dangling a worm in the water. But those who fish with a fly rod—a long, flexible fishing pole—know better.

As the fisherman moves the rod forward, the potential energy in the line behind him changes to kinetic energy. The line forms a *U* as it moves forward.

A successful fly fisher is able to cast, or throw, a tiny artificial fly to a specific spot on a lake or stream. Such a cast depends on the quick **acceleration** of the fly rod followed by a quick stop.

During a fly-fishing cast, the fisher raises the rod and then flips the entire line backward, over and behind his head. The weight of the line causes the rod to flex and store potential energy. When the fly fisher moves the rod forward again, the potential energy begins changing into kinetic energy. As that happens, the tip of the rod pulls the entire line forward, and it begins to form a U. The fisher snaps his wrist to stop the rod, and the U unrolls, carrying the fly far out over the water. A perfect fly cast!

a Line is flipped backward, storing potential energy.

b Fisher moves rod forward.

c Kinetic energy takes over; line unfurls.

d Fisher flicks wrist to stop the rod. U unrolls completely.

THE POWER OF GRAVITY

Gravity is the reason why a kicked football doesn't stay aloft and why snowboarders come crashing down on the half-pipe. Gravity is the force that pulls things toward earth.

Forces may be balanced or unbalanced. Two tug-of-war teams pulling equally hard on a rope is an example of a balanced force. An object cannot move when forces are balanced.

Gravity, on the other hand, is an unbalanced force. There is nothing pulling in the opposite direction. When gravity is the only force acting on an object, that object is said to be in **free fall**. An object in free fall accelerates, or gets faster. Athletes are very aware of this, and are always looking for ways to overcome the pull of gravity—on their equipment, and on themselves.

Although Lebron James seems to defy gravity, he's really using the strength of his legs to force his body up off the ground.

COACH'S CORNER

Question: How does Lebron James defy gravity and hang in the air when he dunks?

Answer: Lebron James is no Spider-Man. His powers are no different than those of any other player. How high James jumps depends on how much force his legs generate when he leaves the ground. How long he stays in the air is related to how high he jumps. One thing is certain, however. Gravity will always bring James back to earth.

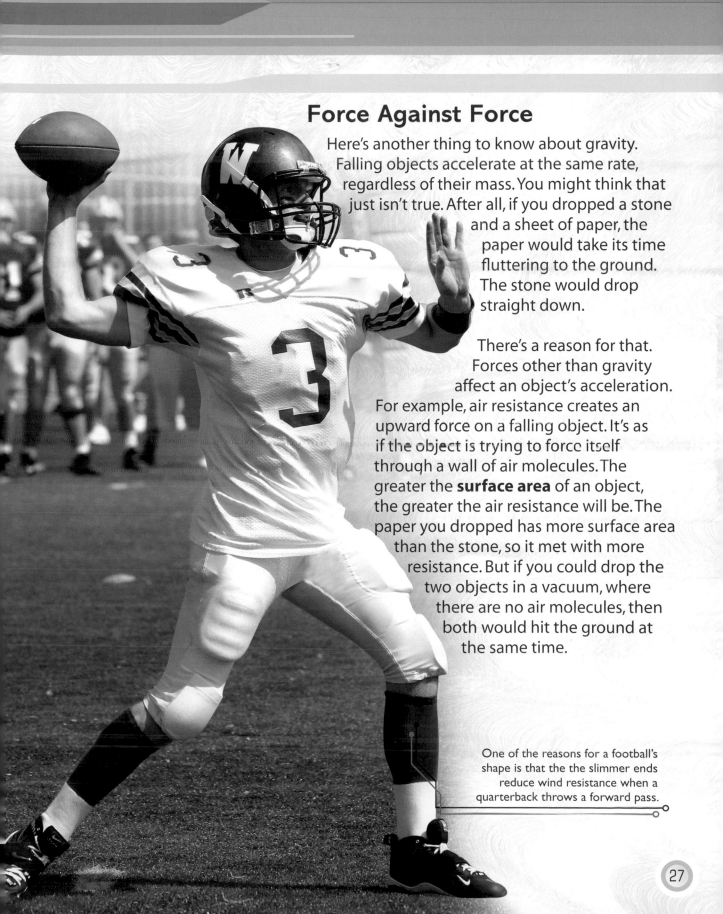

Force Against Force

Here's another thing to know about gravity. Falling objects accelerate at the same rate, regardless of their mass. You might think that just isn't true. After all, if you dropped a stone and a sheet of paper, the paper would take its time fluttering to the ground. The stone would drop straight down.

There's a reason for that. Forces other than gravity affect an object's acceleration. For example, air resistance creates an upward force on a falling object. It's as if the object is trying to force itself through a wall of air molecules. The greater the **surface area** of an object, the greater the air resistance will be. The paper you dropped has more surface area than the stone, so it met with more resistance. But if you could drop the two objects in a vacuum, where there are no air molecules, then both would hit the ground at the same time.

One of the reasons for a football's shape is that the the slimmer ends reduce wind resistance when a quarterback throws a forward pass.

Snowboarding
Gravity on the Half-Pipe

How does a snowboarder control direction and fight the pull of gravity? With friction!

When a snowboarder heads down a slope, a small amount of water forms between the bottom of the moving snowboard and the snow's surface. That water reduces friction between the board and snow. The snowboard moves faster.

That's why snowboarders are always shifting their weight. Each shift causes the board to reduce contact with the snow on one side, while increasing the board's contact with the snow on the other side. This creates friction, and the board changes direction toward the source of least resistance.

Snowboarders control direction by increasing friction on one side of the board.

THE SCIENCE ADVANTAGE

When snowboarders do tricks, they must keep their center of gravity over the edge of the board that is in contact with the snow. The center of gravity is the point of any object where the weight is most concentrated. A snowboarder can crash if he or she tilts even slightly to one side or the other.

Bobsledding

Gravity Goes Downhill

Bobsledding is fast, furious, and a little bit crazy! But gravity is its best friend.

For a bobsled team to win, they need to take advantage of the physical forces that cause the sled to accelerate. They must also reduce the forces that cause the sled to slow down.

Gravity causes all bobsleds to accelerate at the same rate of speed: 32 ft. (9.8 m) per second squared. But if all bobsleds are accelerating at the same speed, why are there winners and losers?

Those who win have bobsleds that reduce the effect of wind resistance. In addition, fast bobsleds have smooth, thin runners that reduce friction.

Getting a good jump off the starting line is also important. The faster the team pushes the bobsled, the quicker its forward movement. This can reduce the impact of air and friction.

Saving even one-tenth of a second during the start can save one-third of a second on the run as a whole—the difference between winning and losing.

THE NEED FOR SPEED

In August 2009 Usain Bolt became the fastest man in the world. He ran the 100-meter dash in 9.58 seconds, shattering the old record of 9.69 seconds. Bolt is fast. But is he speedy?

Usain Bolt holds Olympic records for the 100 meter, 200 meter, and 4 x 100 meter races.

In sports you will often hear speed, acceleration, and velocity used to describe how fast people and objects move. Each of these words means something different. Speed is the rate at which an object moves. The hands of a clock have speed, but no one would say that a clock moves fast. You can calculate the average speed of an object by dividing the distance it has traveled by the time it takes to travel that distance. In other words . . .

$$Speed = \frac{Distance}{Time}$$

COACH'S CORNER

Question: What was Usian Bolt's speed when he broke the 100-meter dash record in 2009?

Answer: If you measure the distance in meters and time in seconds, speed becomes meters per second (m/s). Using the formula, Bolt's speed when he broke the 100 meter record was 10.44 m/s.

But it's not enough to know the speed of something. It's also important to know in which direction the object is moving. Speed in a given direction is called velocity. If you know the speed and direction of a racehorse, you can figure out the animal's velocity.

Then there's acceleration. In the language of sports, acceleration means an increase in speed. But in science, acceleration has a more specific definition. It is the rate at which velocity changes.

Remember, velocity is a combination of speed and direction. Acceleration involves a change in either of these **variables**. Whenever the speed of an object increases or decreases, there is a change in acceleration. Whenever an object changes direction, acceleration changes, as well.

A jockey must control both the horse's speed and its rate of acceleration.

The Luge
Going Down the Tube

Imagine sliding down a slick chute of ice on your back, with nothing more than a fiberglass sled between you and the hard, cold ground. That's what lugers do all the time.

A luge is a small one- or two-person sled. Its riders travel faceup downhill. Velocity plays a big role in the movement of a luge. The faster a luge moves, the farther it will travel in a specific period of time. But as a luge goes down a course, the sled goes through positive and negative velocities.

What does that mean? As it speeds down the track, the luge is said to have a positive velocity. If a luge goes through a turn that takes it in the reverse direction, the luge experiences negative velocity.

As he heads downhill, this luger is experiencing positive velocity.

Springboard Diving

Guo Jingjing is one of China's most admired divers. During the 2008 Summer Olympics in Beijing, Guo won her third and fourth gold medals. The wins made her the most decorated diver in Chinese history.

Acceleration is essential in springboard diving. A diver cannot simply stand on the end of the springboard and expect to achieve the force or acceleration needed to make an Olympic dive.

The strength of a diver's hurdle determines the speed and height of her vertical acceleration.

An expert diver begins a dive by horizontally accelerating—moving forward—from a standing position. When the diver comes to the end of the board, he or she does a hop-skip step called a hurdle. The hurdle gives the diver enough force to accelerate vertically; that is, leap into the air. The arms are then thrown downward to make the upper **torso** parallel with the thighs so the body is in a V shape. Then the diver accelerates downward.

Next, the diver pushes his or her legs toward the sky. That brings the body into the perfect position to splash head first into the water, arms outstretched. The moment the diver hits the water, acceleration slows.

MASTERING MOMENTUM

In professional football, most offensive linemen and fullbacks are over 6 feet (1.8 m) tall, and they weigh more than 290 pounds. Why do coaches look for super-size players?

A popular children's game calls for two teams to line up facing each other. A member from one team runs toward the opposing line and tries to break through. Which players are most successful? The bigger, faster ones.

The reason for this is **momentum**. Momentum means that the more mass an object has, and the faster its velocity, the harder it is to stop. Big, fast football players are hard to bring down when they run. That's why some players are chosen for their size, some for their speed, and some for the ideal combination of both.

Football players use momentum to break through a defensive line.

Jimmie Johnson leading Jeff Gordon during the NASCAR Banking 500 Sprint Cup Series.

Objects can also transfer momentum to one another. Let's say Jimmie Johnson and Jeff Gordon are battling one another at the Lowe's Motor Speedway in Concord, North Carolina. Johnson's car is traveling at 100 meters per second, and Gordon's car is traveling at 50 meters per second. Eventually Johnson's car catches up to Gordon's and bumps into it.

During the collision, the speed of each race car changes. Johnson's car slows down to 50 meters per second and Gordon's car speeds up to 100 meters per second. Johnson's car transferred half of its momentum to Gordon's car. Scientists call that process the **conservation of momentum**.

THE SCIENCE ADVANTAGE

Since momentum is the combination of mass and velocity, increasing either one can give an athlete an advantage. A heavier bat or racquet can move a ball forward with more force. But a faster swing can do the same thing. Each athlete has to decide whether to depend on the weight of the equipment, the strength and speed of his or her swing, or a combination of the two.

Billiards

In 2009, Indian player Pankaj Advani became one of the youngest contestants to win the World Billiards Championship. The physics of momentum has a lot to do with Advani's success.

The game of billiards—as well as other games known as "cue sports" — revolves around angles, velocity, and the transfer of momentum. When a player makes his or her shot, the cue stick transfers energy to the cue ball. The cue ball accelerates and builds momentum. When it strikes the second ball, the cue ball transfers momentum to that ball and sends it toward the pocket.

Advani may also put spin on the cue ball by striking it off center. This means that when the momentum is transferred, the second object will go off in a different direction. Learning to predict these angles is essential to the game.

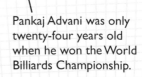

Pankaj Advani was only twenty-four years old when he won the World Billiards Championship.

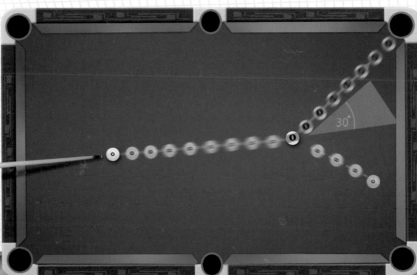

Skateboarding

Try this experiment. Stand in an open space. Jump into the air. While you are airborne try turning your body 90 degrees—a quarter turn—in either direction. Were you successful?

If you were, what you experienced is angular momentum. With angular momentum, a person or object rotates around an axis. (An axis is an imaginary line running down the center of something.) With angular momentum, a rotating skateboarder will keep rotating unless a twisting force, known as torque, acts to stop him.

When rotating in midair, skateboarders twist their arms and torso in one direction, and their legs in the opposite direction. The rotation of the legs and torso cancel each other out. In other words, the skateboarder's total momentum does not change. That's why skateboarders can seemingly defy gravity and hang in the air as they rise off a ramp.

A skateboarder can execute what's called a frontside 180 by twisting his or her torso in midair.

HARD TO RESIST

Athletes don't just compete against one another. They also compete against the forces of nature. One of the ways to beat Mother Nature is through aerodynamics.

In science, aerodynamics is the study of how air moves. In sports, aerodynamics relates to the movement of air and other fluids around a projectile, such as a soccer ball, cyclist, javelin, or race car. Aerodynamics is very important for swimmers, skiers, and sprinters. Any of them can lose a race by fractions of a second if **drag**—the force of air or liquid pushing against them—slows them down.

Sprinters reduce drag by leaning forward as they run.

What causes drag? Drag is a force created by the movement of an object over a distance. For drag to happen, a solid body must be in contact with a liquid or gas. Swimmers create drag when they move through water. Race cars create drag when they move through air.

Drag is at its greatest when the area is large. For example, a missile's slim design helps it reduce the effects of drag far better than does the shape of an airplane. Like a missile, an athlete overcomes the force of drag through a process called **streamlining**. Streamlining minimizes the resistance created by flowing air and fluids around an object.

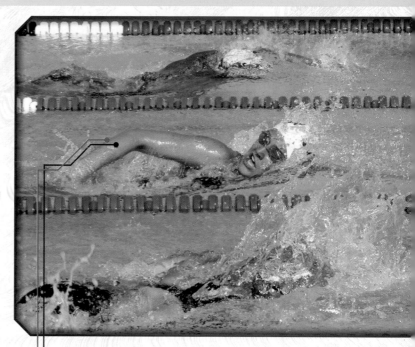

Swim caps and specially designed suits can reduce drag as a swimmer moves through the water.

THE SCIENCE ADVANTAGE

The elliptical shape of a football reduces drag if the quarterback's pass is well thrown. A good quarterback will throw a pass in a tight spiral (spin) around an axis that runs lengthwise through the center of the ball. If the spin axis is off even a bit, drag will cause the ball to wobble. In a perfect pass, the football's spin axis maintains a 10-degree angle along its entire flight path.

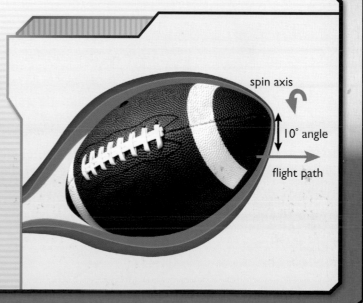

spin axis

10° angle

flight path

Swimming

World-class swimmers such as Michael Phelps make swimming look easy. But drag tries to slow him down with every stroke.

Phelps, like most swimmers, overcomes the effects of drag by being in great physical shape and using equipment that will minimize the effects of drag. In addition, swimmers often shave their bodies. Shaving makes a swimmer's body more aerodynamic because it removes hair and a layer of dead skin cells, which resist a swimmer's forward momentum.

A swimmer's technique can also cut down on drag. The more streamlined a swimmer becomes in the water, the less drag he or she creates in the water.

THE SCIENCE ADVANTAGE

One of the things that make Michael Phelps such a great swimmer is the "dolphin kick." Phelps moves his ankles in a series of flops at the start of each race and while making turns. The technique allows Phelps to stay underwater longer, eliminating drag caused by waves in the pool.

One of a swimmer's goals is to find ways to reduce the drag of the water on his or her body.

Speed Skating

In speed skating, athletes race around a track of ice as quickly as possible. Some go as fast as 30 miles (48 km) per hour!

Only three things can slow these skaters down: the friction between skates and ice, the athlete's own physical endurance, and wind resistance. Skates can reduce friction. Training takes care of endurance. But what can be done about wind resistance?

Skaters keep their bodies low when they race to minimize drag and help them accelerate. Speed skaters also need to have strong legs because they are constantly shifting weight from leg to leg to generate the force that enables them to speed down the track.

In addition, just as swimmers do, speed skaters wear special, skintight suits to become more streamlined and minimize drag. Canadian speed skaters may even go into a **wind tunnel** to figure out which suit will make them more aerodynamic.

The position of this skater's arms adds to the streamlined posture that cuts down on wind resistance.

THE HUMAN MACHINE

Newton's laws, the Bernoulli Effect, momentum, drag— all of these are important to athletes. But their own bodies and technique are the most important factors of all.

All the science in the world doesn't help athletes unless their bodies are in great shape. Organs, bones, muscles, **tendons**, joints, and **ligaments** must all be in peak condition. If one part is not working right, then the entire system may suffer.

Gymnasts require strength, flexibility, and coordination.

What does this mean to the athlete? It means that diet, exercise, and sleep are as important to success as the right equipment and a working knowledge of physics. A linebacker in football needs a body that will withstand the forces generated by constant tackling. A runner or swimmer needs to be able to maintain a fast pace for as long as the race lasts.

42

A golfer builds club velocity through careful execution of the backswing, swing, and follow through.

It's not enough to be in great physical shape, though. All the parts must work together in just the right way. The arms, hips, legs, and torso of a golfer must work together to hit a golf ball far and straight. A baseball pitcher will not last long in a game unless his legs, arms, wrists, and torso do exactly the right thing at the right time.

That's why athletes, coaches, and trainers study biomechanics, which applies the laws of mechanics and physics to how people perform. At the highest level of sports, a player's technique can decide who wins and who loses.

A pitcher's technique includes everything from how the ball is held to the movement of the arm, legs, and torso.

Working Out

Every muscle in the body has one job to do—contract. Whether it is curling a 10-pound (4.5-kilogram) dumbbell or raising a hand in class, a body's skeletal muscles can only contract by the effort of a person's will.

To make the body's muscles perform more efficiently, athletes often work out with weights. Weight training is also known as resistance training. The amount of muscle mass in the body increases as the muscles work harder.

The cells of the body react to the extra resistance by becoming bigger and stronger. That allows the muscles to contract more efficiently. The more muscle you have, the more energy your body burns to function properly. Resistance training also improves the heart and circulatory system.

Athletes plan their weight-training routines to target different muscle groups.

COACH'S CORNER

Question: Do I have to use dumbbells and barbells when I do resistance training?

Answer: You can use your own body weight as resistance by doing pushups, sit-ups, and squats. You can also do isometric exercises to build strength. In addition to building muscle, strength exercises also help burn calories.

Technique

In October 2009, American Kayla Williams won the vault title at the world gymnastics competition. Yet just five months earlier, the sixteen-year-old would not have considered competing at such a world-class level. What had improved? Her technique.

Technique is the way a task or activity is performed. Williams's vault begins with Williams running toward the vault table. As she runs, her arms stay bent close to her side. Legs, feet, and elbows point to the front. This allows her to build up as much speed and force as possible.

Hitting the springboard changes Williams's forward momentum to upward momentum. At this point, Williams makes sure her arms are low and her knees slightly bent so she doesn't lose any power. As Williams hits the table with her hands, her body remains tight. Forward momentum is interrupted, and her body flips over the vaulting table. If she does all of this correctly, the final stage of the vault—the post-flight and landing— will be successful.

In these vaults as with almost every sport—technique is everything.

The arched front layout drill is used by gymnasts to improve their front handspring technique.

GLOSSARY

acceleration The rate at which velocity changes.

aerodynamics The study of how air moves.

air resistance Friction experienced by falling objects.

biomechanics The study of how physics and mechanics apply to human performance.

conservation of momentum When a moving object interacts with another, the total momentum of both objects does not change.

drag The resistance to a moving body created by rushing air.

force Anything that influences the motion of an object.

free fall The motion of an object when gravity is the only force acting on it.

friction The force that one surface exerts on another when the two rub against each other.

gravity The force of attraction between two objects.

ligaments Strong, flexible tissues that connect bones to joints.

mass The amount of matter that makes up an object.

momentum The force, speed, or energy gained by a moving object.

physics The branch of science concerned with laws governing the structure of the universe.

streamlining Designing objects to minimize the resistance of air flow around that object.

surface area The outside or uppermost area of something.

tendons Flexible tissue that joins muscle to bone.

torso The upper part of the body, excluding neck and limbs.

variables Any factor that can change in an experiment.

velocity Speed in a given direction.

wind tunnel A research tool used to study the effects of air moving past solid objects.

FIND OUT MORE

Books

Gay, Timotu. *The Physics of Football*. New York: HarperCollins, 2005. Learn about the physics that govern football and examine some of the sport's most memorable moments.

Goodstein, Madeline P. *Sports Science Projects:The Physics of Balls in Motion*. Berkeley Heights, NJ: Enslow Publishers, Inc., 2008. Exciting experiments explain the physics behind the design and function of equipment from ping-pong balls to footballs.

Levine, Shar, and Leslie Johnstone. *Sports Science*. New York: Sterling Publishers, 2006. A book of activities that explains the science behind everything from baseball and basketball to surfing and swimming.

Websites

www.exploratorium.edu/sports
This website details how science plays a role In such sports as snowboarding, baseball, hockey, and surfing. Many online activities and webcasts are available.

www.soccerballworld.com/Physics.htm
Check out this site if you want to apply the laws of physics to soccer. It explains what happens when someone kicks a soccer ball and the aerodynamics of a moving soccer ball.

www.nas.nasa.gov/About/Education/Racecar/aerodynamics.html
This website from the National Aeronautics and Space Administration (NASA) details the science behind car racing.

INDEX